The Always

Robin Reagler

FlowerSong Press
Copyright © 2025 by Robin Reagler

ISBN: 978-1-963245-25-7

Published by FlowerSong Press
in the United States of America.
www.flowersongpress.com

Author Photo Credit: Tish Gilbert
Cover Image Credit: Lauris Rozentals
Cover Design Credit: Tish Gilbert
Cover Layout & Design Credit: Carlos Fidel Espinoza
Typesetting: Carlos Fidel Espinoza
Set in Adobe Garamond Pro

NOTICE: SCHOOLS AND BUSINESSES
FlowerSong Press offers copies of this book at quantity discount with
bulk purchase for educational, business, or sales promotional use.

For information, please email the Publisher
at info@flowersongpress.com.

Edward Vidaurre
Publisher/Editor-in-chief
FlowerSong Press
www.flowersongpress.com

Dedication

In memory of my parents,
David Reagler and Joanne Davis Reagler

Epigraph

Forever - is composed of Nows -

Emily Dickinson

Contents

Intuition

It begins in my hands.
The idea, a perfect greenness, speeds
up my pulse. I feel it, radioactive throb
in my wrists. The endpoint of loneliness
is to escape the living. I do not mean
to stare into this wilderness.
Above me, miles of angry
sky. Like a secret stored inside
the body's cells. Like having a crush on
the secret *you*. Like my mother, shrinking
more each day, still telling me which hill
to climb and do I hear her? Am I near
enough? Because just this once
I have no doubt: when she dies
we all die with her.

Questions of Residence

To be with a dying person
is to inhabit a different world
from this one. This one with
nights and days, freeways
and breaking news. And once
that person dies, say, your
mother, for instance, it's
yet another world again,
one with cake and kids,
pets and jobs, but they are
pale like mist, almost invisible.
Laughter is a soundtrack,
and love is a song played on
your neighbor's violin. Favorite
meals taste like the earth,
and kissing leads only
to dashing out of the house
crying, bewildered, sitting
alone on the front steps.
Or maybe the back. In this world
there are so many more hours
in each day. People often wish
for more time, but I think time
is undoing me. The moon

conspires with all the ever-
greens. There is no guessing
what these trees might do
to me in the next flurry
of stage five hurricanes.
Heaven is just a feather
of a word. I wonder who
I am in this new place. I wonder
how it would feel to meet her now.
Would anger or sorrow or sadness
swim up from my insides? Eyeing
the broken parts of terra cotta
on the porch, I ask myself
about the broken.
Nobody knows how.
Nobody knows why.

The Way

I know, while peeling the clementines

for them, that they are ripe. The way fingernails

grow secretly or not at all. The way

she says the word terraces, and it sounds

like terrorists. The way smoke travels

lazily from one mouth to another.

The way stories bleed as they sing.

The way the cat sleeps in my spot

on the bed, with his head half-hidden

beneath his shadowy paw. The way I pray

sleep will drape itself over me like a living

mountain of curtain. The way I die

with my father every night, over and over,

holding his dry and weightless hand.

The Hiding Place

Our children dream of doves
ghost-floating in the sky.
A cold emptiness invades
our heads. All our messages
to one another are made
of dust. The gardener is talking
pansies, talking mulch. I might
be that gardener, it isn't
clear. Hoes and shovels lean
haphazardly against the fence. I am
wondering what to do now, what
to do next. The children marvel over
a pony that's wandered across
the fields. Its holiness couldn't
be more obvious. Pony-breath
appears as steam in the air. I say
the word *death* and taste salt
in my mouth. Since the sun's
wrapped in red paper, we fold it
into origami stars that begin
to burn. We hear something.
The thunderous stampedes
come closer, and we hide

beneath the stairwell, together,

holding hands in the dimness.

There is no lust like the lust

of the religious crusaders, so we make

ourselves very small and hold our breath,

longing for the beloved assassin.

Until Dawn, Barbaric

My mother dies on occasion,
looping toward her extinction.
Each time she returns to me
in a new version. She speaks
slowly, the syllables sweeping, as
though she's unaware of the pansies
blooming inside her throat. But
she knows they're there. She
nurtured them as they grew.
Tonight her battered voice
sings *sotto voce* from her very
bones, introducing me to
a music that can only be described
in the imagery of Arkansas:
deer night-grazing in the meadow.
You eat the glow of dark songness.
Because of their eyes. Their eyes.

Kaddish for my Father

I keep remembering what wasn't said

I hold onto a word until it makes me sick

like a bright worm inside my intestines.

The blindness of my father

devolving from eyes to ex-eyes,

one replaced by a glass replica

has me bending my guilt into

pages, pounding the January air

into ash, a gallery of spent, a

pastry made of clay.

Into the empty city, I

speed along without destination,

letting night be my

candle, driving the car into

the heat of my sadness, imagining

myself hanging from an oak

by my long hair like Absalom,

oh Absalom, I cry out

like a wild, imperfect daughter-son.

Coma

Why am I here
My head is bleeding for no reason
That is not my mother
I make myself touch her
      although I am afraid

She is not dying
Not at all dying
How would I know?
Her lips look bruised
Her toes, wrong and blue
Systems are failing
My hands don't know how to act
Do you hear ashes
The sound of horses stomping
The shadows lost in her lungs,
      knocking to get out

There is something
There is nothing
Now, now, and now
A child playing scales on a tiny violin

The Always of Grief

In grieving, I have flown

I have flown out of myself

I have flown over highways and billboards, wide rivers and red clay bluffs

I have felt my love flow into flowers, I've watched them bloom

I have embraced the *the* and carried it, a pearl of sorts, to the edge of sound

At the very edge, the mourning tree spreads its ever widening

      arms and speaks in recurring dreams

Dreams that have been simplified to their most basic elements

Cloud, train, fire, door

There at the edge my

Sense of what I've lost

Is a tiny wren, a feather, my sense

Of praise for

The nest of us

Grief. Sex. Mourning.

There was no twang in the system   so I hurled it

into the fire   My mother kept scratching

an itch that infuriated   every cell of her

dying   which for her must have been

a kind of perhaps   a kind of dry fire   a burning

with death   the only possible

healing

      No doubt I am guilty

as hell   for this human interpretation

Or else you must see me   so clearly that like the flow of electrons

that completes the circuit   this

is an ending, this is   all there is

I will   ask you a question

you already   memorized your   answer

Desire cripples me

you know   what I need

I am humble   humiliated   fueled

by my own despair   as I beg you

I beg you

lust instructs me   and there's a turntable, with   that scat song

repeating the pain   repeating the pain

a rhythmic

witness to this   most recent test of our love

fastening, unfastening   the already pounding of

our bodies

Desire Diary

Inside the mechanism, everyone

        was handsome. Everyone

Came at it with a strange green

        sound leaking from their

Lips. At 4 a.m. she sensed a classic

        case of slash and burn.

It was decided, she would be slash,

        I, burn. In this way

Generosity became organized into

        compartments, and we

Could take turns reading

        the ransomed air.

Which is to say. Now we lie on our backs

        in the hotel bed catching

Our breath thinking that nothing

        is as pure as this nothingness,

While the sash of sleep coils around

      our lips and wrists, binding

Us, the pure, the forgetful

      we were when this

Ritual began. It's how—

      around, and down—

we end up where we began.

Deep inside me, the hawks

Are circling. Again. Their
Single-mindedness blitzes in
And prepares for some kind
Of fight. With effort I manage
To control my face, but I
Carefully avoid the cameras.
I walk as though I am
Not completely visible. When
I arrive before you, it is as
An acolyte, waiting to be
Taught. I dream of escaping
The terror that I might
Simply become. There are many
Ways to tell any story.
Fear. Desire. Fire.
My body is the lesbian body.
And when in darkness you
Come to me, I struggle
To believe you're real.
Then I, the self who is
Nobody, begin to burn,
And I am lit up and wed
To the fields on fire.
That is called flying,
And there is nothing
Like it. Nothing before
It. Nothing after it.

The Lesbian Body

Is a haunted

house that frightens

me. It is

An open-

ended question.

Desire

Terrifies

me. I think

of the indifferent

Blue

of jellyfish

in an aquarium.

I think

about their beauty,

their border-shifting

Bodies,

breathing,

seething,

At one

with the water

surrounding them.

And I think

about how

I disappointed

You

and then

you died.

The Cutting Hour

More nowhere than a fever

Stronger than a sparrow

The song of the railroad train

Lulls us to sleep if you listen

Yes, the first evening knows

The heart knows early on

The blood cells scream out knowledge

And falling   not falling   falling again

I am   we are   you will be

Like a tourniquet, mostly alive

At the border of two stories

Re-routed

I am not you. Just placed here by you. My body that came from your
       bodies.

The prayer *Kaddish* enters me, a bullet between my teeth. Briefly, all
       my cells

can curse. Then you both disappear, traveling a road that was never
       there. As in

calculus, the road becomes a non-place in steady motion. It is

       represented by

the letter Y.

Upward,

outward,

skyward.

And we,

opening

our eyes,

are surprised by the incandescence that outlines every mountain,
       every rugged tor.

Grief creates its own fire. Its own revelation. My parents, two silver
       dots on a temporary

paper map. And traveler, although we have only just met, your fate is
         mine. Once fate

flares up into horizon, you will understand why I am taking
         another crash course in dust

signaling

pathways

for the dead,

as the skinny

child

is running

through

the fields, brandishing a willow branch and condemning the beauty
         of a perfect day.

Binge Grieving

You answered the question
why pain causes bodies to contract
why bodies speak their strange languages
yet to think (wool-brained, looping)
about erasing distances between lovers
to become dazzling, only to disappear
I'm rope-tied to my story
of my father dying each day
my mother clicking, then burning
my mouth fills with imaginary feathers
my heart rattles
guilty as gun shot
wishes become bells
while sleep spools out its message
magenta and clotted
my brain as a dog
my love as soap, salt, sunshine
dumping me in a place
where I am kissed
into blindness I am
ever-unfolding in your absence

Alternate Names for G-d

Rock

Rocked

                              Clock House

Duck decoy   Brakes

                                                        Outer space

Lob

Fake lake   Grief

Pop of comic   Book

                              Drop cloth

Boomerang   Blame

                                                        Love-proof

Asleep in an Instant

Mobility   From Earth

                              From fire

Sanctuary, or I'm Bleeding

Because I sleep face-down, I am

night's sister, I am death's husband,

I am the whore of the Lord. I wake up

sore and tired, remembering a girl

in France. I watch her sitting

upright on the wooden pew singing

a psalm that expresses all that I am

      grief   sex   mourning

      fear   desire fire

in a medieval church. Why has she

come for me? The wind, the naked

wind, has a voice that ticks. I am

alone, and the long line of time

ceases to breathe. Sunrise will never

arrive. Squinting, I wish for hell. It swims up

brightly and fills me with wonder.

I Try to Talk about my Body

I peel away layers,

father, mother, lover, family, career, blades

of Arkansas   I peel away

the cousinry   the country roads

I peel away friend upon friend

because in the hope to become pure

I adopt a rescue dog   the dog rescues me

Instead of making my own choices, I follow

yellow arrows down a path

to soothe both   anger and angst

I suppose: this body is

layers of living matter

and just as I had hoped (fingers

crossed) to be protected

by that accretion over time

but in the process of stripping

my nesting-doll self   down,

I discover the same naivete of childhood

the rawness and vulnerability

the shock of the first assault

as though those layers were not

created from within but painted onto me

Then: hell-weather and

rain, rain, they're gone away

like how you take off a pair of gloves

like how you undress,

hoping, as you crawl into bed

hoping to develop some trust

and to glow   from within

as she does

like the quiet sturgeon moon

Poem that I Can't Finish

Today I didn't write you

because I was mind-muddled

with the sounds of the railroad

trains in the yard I refused

to sign my name I

felt my limbs as though

they weren't really mine

and in a moment of double vision

having forgotten to eat

I began to write

so here's a poem for

the emptiness of days

when the body remembers

exactly what it can or will contain,

like an addition problem

without an actual total

Am I lonely? I ask

my lungs. *Aren't I ready?*

I ask my legs.

Because although I make myself

love-proof, I won't be touched

in that way again, I will never

touch you in that way. I

am a promise. This is

a poem about the story

you never told me. It's

the untold stories with gigantic

hawk wings that swoop back over me

darkening the breathable air

and turning to dirty steam, the speed

of that memory, illegal,

the tell as I walk alone along

the train tracks, ignoring the pennies

stretched to three times their size,

looking upward to greet

the bellowing thunderstorm that never

Grief and Other Addictions

After both parents   died

she did not   know.

She walked around   saying

I don't know I don't   *know.*

And she could hear   herself

breathing and nobody   could

look at her and she got   vertigo

and was afraid to   talk

to even the ones who   knew her

best The party that   is

the universe   stopped

each time she   entered

Constellations shifted   Where

the moon had been   sitting

a bright hole   punch

of the sky They   said

it would get   better

They all said   that

Thorns

Some days I am an atheist
taking a crash course in dust.
The cold seeps into the house
through the windows and hard-
wood floors. In sentences. In cold
hard sentences I think about
my mother, even when
I'm not thinking about her
at all. She and her body
that isn't hers any more.
I feel fear in my teeth,
then my childhood blooms.
I'm the boy prince of every
weed and bug in the gullies.
My brother and I know
each dip and ditch of this.
Now my brother is laughing,
and I'm racing uphill with a swarm
of hornets forming a crown
in my hair. Stung dozens
of times, the pain flips
over and spills out
across the kitchen table.
I am eleven. Mom makes
a paste of water and baking

soda and rubs it into my
head. It dries white in my
black curls. She leaves me
to dry in sunshine. You weren't
there, although I'd begun
to imagine you. And now? I can't
stop thinking about your hands.

Time Is Not a Line

Skies are flying. I, wild
As the flowers, wild
As birds escaping

Sudden knowledge.
Somehow it's been a year
Since we planted my father

Into this hill, and somehow
I keep hurting myself without
Meaning it. Pain is G-d's

Season too. Clouds rake the sky,
And I taste the thunder,
Almost metallic, like

Clams. If I feel fine,
Why do my ears keep
Bleeding. What is the

Noise coming from that raft
Of hot air. Lightning
Clears a path for us.

There. I am breathing
Again. But mesmerizing
Me, terribly far away,

My father's tombstone.
Am I still able to assemble
His voice, his face.

Memory's drumming
Carries a message to us, the
Mourners. We are

Clocks within hearts
As we glide through
The January graveyard.

Dear Knuckles

Dear widening circle scar on my hand that began at my mother's funeral

Scar starting at the base of my thumb

to enforce my remembering

The body's natural tattoo

Dear circle on the date that she died

Circle on the date of the funeral

Circle of relatives round the rectangular 8 x 3 hole in the cold Arkansas earth

Feel this as winter

Dear witness

Dear fake flower of making do

Terra cotta objects marking the grave beside my father's tombstone

Which is now their shared tombstone

In death as in life

I am memorizing the graveyard

And thinking about the old song travelin' shoes

As a machine lowers my mother down into the earth

Thump when the coffin reaches the bottom

Clanking of someone riding a bad bike on the road beside the
    cemetery

Shift of my mother's small body moving inside the coffin

Smell of dead January

Nearby grave with ugly tablecloth made of pure petroleum products
    that will outlast the all of us

Dear Always

Always traveling toward brittle

Always something wrapped in plastic

Forgetting the words of the Kaddish prayer

Hiding tears from my kids and siblings

Because I am now

Because I am dead to the living

Dead to the dead

Buried in cold sunshine

The brilliance

Boutonnière

With the black bandage wrapped three
times around my index finger
where I burned, let me be lookout
for the all of us, for the nest,
bitter, better
luck next time,
finally, I feel sideways
the internal jazz
that yanks me off the ledge
of my own desires which are
sizable and I

tethered to finality
brave the dry
heaves of goodbye as my mother's
velvety maroon shirt
can be seen just
barely through the open crack
of the casket lid, as I peer
down into the rectangular
mouth of earth. My love
for her is shaped like rebellion.
She always drew the one,
and she knew it. It's been 2,
nearly 3 years, and I feel

my grief in my teeth, the back

molars, to be specific, and pain

is just a container, isn't it?

to hold the starch in

its creases. I remember

the lines in her face,

how she held her jaw:

my face, my jaw. I play

the mirror, having fought

against her

waking and sleeping,

all our lives and now

pinned to my lapel

I wear her every word.

Her Absence

If my mother is dying,
I lose my nerve in the dark
If she is, she is everything
conspiring, conditional
If she is not, she will be
threading a needle
and darning the holes
in my body. Her absence is
pain, escalating. I'm closing
down, although it's
a terrible idea. How is love
possible if she's gone.
A migraine plays
riptide in my head.
It seems important
to let go of what I've been
unable to release if I can.
I open myself to something
I cannot imagine something I
don't understand something
like a nest filled with stars.
It is almost morning.
I open myself to the newness
that was not possible before.
I open myself to you.

Kaddish for My Mother

She swims in through my mouth
I feel the hum of her in my teeth

Not sure what they mean by death
Because she's more here now than ever

For one more night I'll harbor you,
I tell her, but she's never been fooled

By ultimatums, especially mine,
Childish and wishful and prayed

She is what zooms through me,
The brand that names me daughter,

And without her there, I'm a mere
Machine, the quiver of my jaw

Gives me away and what can I say
That will release her into the next

Remarkable world? I recite the words
To unlock some secret blessing.

When it finally works, I'll let you
Know, but it might take time.

Meanwhile I tilt and rise,
A bottle floating in both

Oceans, bearing a scrawl
I can't yet interpret

Nobody's Children

It's impossible to predict

Cloud-shaped names   Pillow names

how the stranded feel regret

and they don't realize they are hunted

Destiny names   Linear names

Their desire is expressed in precise

parallel lines cut into their forearms

Camouflage names   Commando names

Transcending from pain to lightness

to a forced steadiness of breath

Remaining names   Becoming names

as their bodies unreel a list of what

we have lost that can never be replaced

So, Ocean

You take a wretched gulp
as sea gulls rifle out sound
where I buried my hair
in sand and ever since
then we, cascading,
agree that we
are now euphemisms

Bring on your dangerous
Bring absurdity and prickly ridicule
What do I know of riptide
Bring purpose and palm fronds
Graying bones and dead ropes
I have nothing to lose says
the motherless motherless
voice spewing out of my mouth

The Thread

I used to be somebody's daughter.
When sadness threatens to take me down, the rituals
kick in. I begin
by walking it out.
Sadness, the thread,
I, the spool.

Sunshine hits metal
The brightness, blinding

I want you to understand how I feel
[We pause inside this poem together]

Without Rules

She has taken to scouring the moon

      Thus the clean streaks change nightly

The surface distressed to the Nth degree

      Soon it will burst, smithereens careening

While stars, like pendants, vanish into orange

      I know because I don't sleep

The heart is a goat that will eat anything

I wake up the rooster at sunrise

      To watch the new day being born

Blue flickers flaming shyly into gold

      After coffee I get to work

Digging for bells buried in yard

      Please ignore the holes surrounding

The tulip tree that will be filled

      By weather's months, then years

I Am Kneeling

People who do not tell their stories
keep quiet to tighten up time.
I haven't suffered as much as you.
My thoughts are wrong and hardly mine.
In dreams you are pregnant, and as I hold
my palm to the globe of your belly,
fear stiches my mouth shut.
When it comes to us, I am confused.
The ocean is human is a flying among stars.
My mother has left behind her living
body, and it somehow knows my name.
I haven't suffered as much as you.
On TV there's always a new disaster
with people shouting lies and
shooting bullets at one another.
I'm not sure why I love you.
In the park my aloneness does
not stand out so much.
Dogs sniff each other, then play.
How is it they know what they know?
I walk for hours until I can't any more,
kicking dust from earth to heaven.
All the park benches, empty, and over-
head the hawks circle us without any
effort, as though it's the easiest way.

Some Days, Ophelia

She looked in the mirror there was her mother she looked again she was playing a violin the pain echoed her loss threw pebbles at the painted clouds parents die leaving us haunting us here is Ophelia somebody needs to do something somebody who could touch her in a way that says "cradle" the moon is so tiny I can barely see faith breaks into shatters in slow motion and the reflection is disguised as her mother her love shot out of a cannon not a ball but a sleeping baby she looks again and there is her mother lost and labored breath celebrating echoes I have a bad feeling about desire which once kept me alive and hopeful yet in every cell of our bodies we are subjects and where is the king where is the map an old man takes a nap on a postage stamp this is all a trick a dream wake me up right now where are all the women we depend on each other our collective potential is empire we're not playing any more the corpses blanket the stage which turns into stone which turns into story the desire tilting upward and rising so that you reach a point where you can look down on your mother who is kneeling below you and you are missing her so much it hurts you're waiting for her although the actors take a bow it's over you're talking to the sliced moon straining to brighten a dull yellow sky and now outside the only way out diving into the freezing cold just because it would be better to feel something anything everything else

Romance

Now is the time of night I miss her most.
I stare at my wrists, feeling the pain pulse,
my life, her death, my life, her death,
and my ankles know the same old crippling.
Inevitably, I am falling. Now is the time,
and I'm this girl-boy-child groping for
a doorway in the dark. I remember feeling
the fabric of the dresses in her closet and moving
toward her too, although she wasn't like that
with me and her breath that smelled of scotch.
She didn't like being touched, I finally realize.
When I was in college, she'd come visit me
in New Orleans, and we'd drink in the bars
where my dad had courted her. We'd walk
through the quarter holding hands, laughing.
The porn stars and drag queens did their thing.
I loved it way too much, I guess. And towards
morning we'd drink black coffee at a café
near the Mississippi, and the caffeine woke
me up like a slap on the cheek, and I knew
myself and pretended it was going to be okay.

Hellbent

History is a body
      of water. I
am a body driven
      by desire. Skin
reminds us of the limits
      of love. Everything
hurts. Missing her is a form
      of destiny, a trial.
What do I mean by that?
      I am bored and too
alone, sitting in silt and porn and pain and breath.
      The temptation to create
dramatic physical sensation
      of any kind
to distract us from what's absent
      rules, and let's
face it, the complete foolishness of confession.

Perhaps

Hurricane Harvey, 2017

As the power gave out, the generator kicked in
As rain fell, I felt her ghost escaping through a window
Vanishing into green dusk
As the pet dog found its inner watch dog
I dragged both mutts across the mushy field of weeds
Helicopters buzzing above, filming us
And the rain fell and continued falling
In an endless loop of rainfall
And I honestly wondered if perhaps it wouldn't end

If perhaps I should open my mouth
Wide to catch it as it came down and down

At night I never slept
There was nothing to be done
When we made love it was more about fear
And placing a barrier between ourselves
And the future which had become THE FUTURE
As I catalogued the details of the real
As real as the hand that glides into her
As real as the mouth that takes her on these shores

And with waves crashing down upon us I told her

A story

A story about simple times

A story erasing the story I believed was true

Because believing came down to this

And only this:

We are wind swept

Sex as Communication

Motility

             Inertia

Eclipse

Moot Court   Language

             Anger

Twang

Desire

Desired

Teeth   Awake in the Forest

Owl   Uneven screech

Moon   Sharpened edge

The Uncanny

I am easily confused—did she die
      or was it me? We're surrounded
by faces that I'm no longer able
      to read. Each night seems darker,
and I'm afraid of walking here alone.
      If I'm honest, the only
thing I'm looking for is love, and I
      may not recognize it when it
arrives. Street lamp above wet stone, wrist
      watch with a green glow. Why
am I how would I who do I, in a cyclone
      of not-knowing. Rabbits sing
their secrets to you and only you.
      I walk up from behind and wrap
my arms around your waist, lonely
      breath at your neck, and I hold
you for longer than I probably should.

The Dead Stalk Us

Someone is following you tonight, but fret

      Not. It's just my mom on the haunt.

She left all her sneakiness behind

      When she died. If you listen

Closely, her footsteps chime, there's data

      In every echo. Walk as though

You are asleep, whisper love songs

      To yourself, and you'll be fine.

Neighbors are taking turns trailing you

      Both, making sure you're safe.

Overhead there's an astronaut orbiting

      Planet Earth. Let that be me,

Magnetized to you both, as I truly am.

      Now you glide into the open

Field, hands deep in the pockets of your

      Dress. You want so much

To turn around, offer her an arm to steady

      Her in her trek, but that can't

Be. So instead you look for the bird

      Nest that is her obituary, the willow

Tree that is her legacy, and into the sky. Please

      Know that I am up here, half

To blame for my own phantom madness,

      Drowsy with passion I never knew was

Mine, keeping my desire a secret, even

From myself. From the sky,

The blurring shapes sharpen.

My dead mom winds her way

Through these nights. Shelter her

Until she's ready to move on.

Yahrzeit

Dear Mother Candle, somehow year
after year there is always so much left
to say. Like the water-to-ice continuum,
I have been investigating the journey
from solid to liquid and back again.
I no longer always feel the heat
of your absence, but sometimes without
realizing it, I notice my fingernails,
torn and bleeding, and I wonder, *how*.
Every morning around 10 am I cough
for an asthmatic hour and then it's gone.
Houston in April, too green and blooming.
The space you once occupied is filled
with blood and coughing. I don't let
anyone see me cry. I write the fastest
words in notebook after notebook.
When I feel empty, I feed the fire inside.
What exactly do I mean by that sentence?
I mean that this morning I didn't know
if I'd be able to get out of bed. But I did.
And tossed into the circus I call a job,
I landed amid laughs and happiness
happening with me in it. With pollen
and songs and poems and sorrow,

What is this busy life that appears to be

mine? Is it bees? Some days I think

I am bees, motivated by one flower

and then another, not sure how things

should happen, in the absence

of queen, in search of the plan.

Alternate Names for Us

On one such flammable night
when the stars no longer conspire
against me, I
arrive at her throat,
lips ready to press my love into skin, to
ignite a blaze in her nerve endings,

and somehow grief swings a 180
so that instead of her, again I'm thinking about my-
self, my mouth swimming inside
hers, my desire erasing
her need from the dashboard of
what-even-is. I

struggle to reclaim some gritty sense of
this woman I love. But it is losing
upon losing, another rendition
of Let's Get Lost. We twist
with violence and beauty
in the rounding-out space
of our one, our single body,
twinning.

The How and the Why

But mostly I think about love.
I think about you. I think about time
as the ocean and our stories as boats
made of paper. The fragility of our stories,
the unlikeliness of love, and the tomboy
certainty of a childhood in Arkansas
where I swallowed back down my fear
and felt things secretly, then not at all.
I think about the ocean, the engineering
within ocean waves. I feel the technicality
of my body as a part of the waves, the pull
and suck of the tides. The moon as a kind
of kindness masterminding the landscape.
I feel *Kaddish*, the Hebrew prayer providing
rhythm for just how the living will remember
the dead. I swear on my own skeleton that
I can see the hidden architecture inside living
things in the natural world. I remember darkness.
I remember my mother, the way she held her jaw
like stone and maintained that rigid grip
even as she was dying. I think about her.
I think about you. And my words as bricks
that sink deeper and deeper, as bricks dreaming
their way back into the earth.

Safe House

Loss is a noun. My dad, my mom, my marriage, my job. Start losing, keep losing, lost. Then before long it's the red plastic sled of childhood, and who knows how fast it will take you down the icy hill. Once I solidly hit the trunk of a tree. It had been a tiny slip of an elm until I rammed into it, and the mind my mind opened with constellations I could not recognize. The questions I answered with I'm okay by rote because I had no idea, I just said the easiest thing to say like thank you come back, and I measure out a portion of snow in each gloved hand the big neighbor boys lifted me up by my parka armpits. I closed my eyes and did not cry. My house was across the street, and Mom felt for lumps on my head that weren't there yet, just the stickiness in my hair. Stay awake, they keep saying to me, stay awake and there will be grilled cheese for lunch and a story book read out loud and you are you, you are you, you are re-entering the dazzle of your own safe house. The blanket, wool, scratchy in a stay-awake way and at first everyone is quiet and then not at all -- mom back to the kitchen assembling sandwiches, my sister playing with the toy Fisher Price villagers, and my brother, age 5, tightening the belt of his blue bathrobe, insisting he is king.

The Always of Love

Is it true that grief brought us together?

That our words, writing to one another, became water?

That in the absence of mothers and lovers,

we slid from two into one?

It has been three pandemical seasons

since we were together, and the distance

between us is paint fading. When I miss you

most, I catalogue the things you love,

tiny seashells grouped in threes, the fields

of deer in Friday Harbor, the haystack rock stark in the Pacific, the
     search

for whales and seals, the campfires on the beach,

the coffee and toast with honey, butter, and salt,

the baby lizards scampering south to north,

the waves of wildflowers bending along the bayou,

your beautiful poems wrapped in red silk

(I unfold the silk—they've disappeared)

There are so many kinds of exile.

I wonder if you know that in the future that I imagine

we are linked in magic and peonies

at a beyondable altar. We are an adventure.

We spin the wheel of the elements.

But for now, like in our earliest days

together, we are apart and

have only our words to bind us.

I send you this poem, my holiest

scroll made only of breath.

A Litmus Test for Faith

I ask for an alphabet,
but nobody hears me.
The singing children
navigate by instinct,
and their song spills
doubt into the atmosphere.
The sky is the problem.
The star, imprisoned
in glee, goes nowhere
for a million years.
Everyone knows that
beauty is temporary.
Sometimes I close my
eyes, pretending I am
blind, like my father
was back when he was.
The world's curtain
brightens inside
the mind's animate eye.
In this way I continue
to surprise myself.
A murmuration
of starlings. A chilly
breeze in June.

We Holy Thieves

At night I write to you
Because the moon's fullness
Is a bad accident, and I
Need to travel halfway
Across Texas, driving
In reverse. Our love
Is a screech owl; we
Agree on that
Much. I'm miles past
Livingston, past
Nacogdoches. The darkness
Gasps with the blush
Of sunrise. Nobody
Recognizes what is
So obviously blooming.
The beautiful part   is you.

Acknowledgments

I would like to express my gratitude to the following editors for publishing these poems in print journals, on radio, and in online magazines: Michael Broder, Catherine Esposito, Jen Karetnick, Anna Leahy, Catherine Lu, Wayne Miller, Caridad Moro-Gronlier, and Mark O'Connor.

Chaos Dive Reunion (book) : *Some Days, Ophelia*

Copper Nickel: *Grief. Sex. Mourning.*

Flush Left: *Dear Always, Intuition, Until Dawn, Barbaric*

Houston Public Radio: *We Holy Thieves*

SLAB: *Perhaps, The Dead Stalk Us, The Thread,*

SWWIM: *The How and the Why*

TAB Journal: *A Litmus Test for Faith, Questions of Residence*

Several of the poems first appeared in *Teeth & Teeth*, winner of the Charlotte Mew Prize, selected by Pulitzer Prize winner Natalie Diaz, and published by Headmistress Press. My heart full of thanks goes to Risa Denenberg and Mary Meriam for their work on that project.

Alternate Names for G-d

Alternate Names for Us

Desire Diary

Grief. Sex. Mourning

I am Kneeling

Nobody's Children

Re-Routed

The Way

We Holy Thieves

Some of the poems included in this manuscript were written at the Helen Riaboff Whitely Center at Friday Harbor Labs, which is run by the University of Washington. Thank you for the time, the beautiful space, and natural beauty of the place.

Many friends have supported me in this project, especially Marcia Chamberlain, my partner of 21 years and mother of our children, Pearl and Carrie. My added gratitude goes out to many others, including my family, my writing group, aka The Matrix, Jane Creighton, Ruth Dickey, Ruth Ellen Kocher, Charlie Scott, Edward Vidaurre, and Cynthia Williams. And profoundly, with joy and love, thank you, Tish Gilbert.

www.ingramcontent.com/pod-product-compliance
Lightning Source LLC
Chambersburg PA
CBHW031247120626
46545CB00007B/2697